Cooking the Movies

50 Recipes
From Iconic Movies

Dereck Moore

CONTENTS

SWEET RECIPES 73

BEVERAGES AND COCKTAIL RECIPES   95

COOKING CONVERSION CHARTS   111

COOKING THE MOVIES!

In movies, everything looks great; that's the magic of cinema. The big screen beautifully captures the two most important senses of vision and hearing. However, it also subliminally stimulates our senses of taste and smell. Breakfast is considered the most important meal of the day, but for movie lovers, the most important meal of the day is the one that is served on the silver screen in front of a packed theater.

Food plays an essential role in telling those great cinematic stories. Food brings any scene alive, with an elegant meal accompanying those handsome actors and beautiful actresses. Everything about movies is mesmerizing, and food is no exception. Food helps tell the stories and brings everything together to create an atmosphere that fascinates the audience. From the fictional Big Kahuna Burger from Pulp Fiction to the shrimp-freak friend of Forrest Gump (Bubba), who can forget those cameo foods that almost took away the limelight from the dashing movie stars?

Familiar with the feeling of getting really hungry while watching your favorite movies, and not knowing why? Well, of course, it might be because you are really hungry… But another intriguing reason is that the foods from those movies send our brains mouthwatering subliminal messages. Thank God they at least serve popcorn at movie marathons!

In this book, we have made a serious attempt to explore the exotic, delicious foods from our all-time favorite movies. Imagine having the same meal on your plate as the characters in those movies are eating; yes, it adds a powerful punch of cinematic flavors!

1

From the emotional Bridget Jones to the dashing James Bond, explore the most popular movie recipes in this special book. These recipes are meant to bring back those golden memories that we have shared with our favorite stars. These are the foods that we've always wanted to eat. And if you're not familiar with some of these movies, that just means it's time to add them to the list. If you're a movie lover, you simply cannot afford to miss those great performances.

So, who says movies can't make you taste or smell something? Savor your meals with these wonderful movie-based recipes that will have you craving more and more.

SAVORY RECIPES

1. Leek Soup from the Movie
Bridget Jones's Diary

Our adorable and beautiful Bridget Jones is an amazing news anchor, but boy she can't cook! She desperately wants to impress her friends by trying her hand at this leek soup, but her plans go awry when she leaves a piece of blue twine in the boiling pot to accidently turn the soup into "blue leek soup". Enjoy this warm soup!

Serves 4 | Prep. time 5–10 minutes | Cooking time 20 minutes

Ingredients

10 medium leeks (white and light-green parts only), sliced and rinsed thoroughly
¼ cup all-purpose flour
¼ cup (½ stick) unsalted butter
1 tablespoon chopped tarragon
Salt and pepper to taste
1 quart low-sodium chicken broth
1 cup water

Directions

1. Slice the leeks to make about 8 cups. Melt the butter in a saucepan over medium high heat.
2. Stir in the leeks and stir-cook for 6–8 minutes to soften. Add the flour and stir-cook for 1 minute.
3. Add the water and broth and bring to a boil.
4. Simmer the mixture over low heat for about 10 minutes, whisking periodically.
5. Add the tarragon and combine well.
6. Transfer the mixture to a blender and puree it.
7. Return the soup to the saucepan and heat again. Season with salt and pepper.
8. Serve warm.

2. Prison Sauce from the Movie Goodfellas

This meat sauce is a product of teamwork by the beloved mobsters Vinnie, Paulie and Johnny in the popular hit Goodfellas. This hearty sauce is for all the Goodfellas fans. Serve with your favorite pasta.

Serves 6–8 | Prep. time 20 minutes | Cooking time 4 hours 20 minutes

Ingredients
Sauce
2 tablespoons olive oil, more if needed
3 pounds veal shanks
3 pounds beef shanks
1 pound Italian pork link sausages, mild or hot
3 small onions, diced thinly

3 cloves garlic, peeled and paper thin sliced
2 tablespoons tomato paste
¼ cup dry red wine
4 (28-ounce) cans Italian tomatoes
1 teaspoon dry basil
1 teaspoon dry oregano
Kosher salt and freshly ground black pepper (to taste)

Meatballs
1 pound ground beef
1 pound ground veal
1 tablespoon Italian seasoning
1 onion, diced thinly
2 garlic cloves, minced
¾ cup regular breadcrumbs
2 large eggs, beaten
½ cup fresh Italian parsley, chopped
1 cup freshly grated parmesan
Salt and freshly ground black pepper

Pasta
1 pound dried spaghetti or other favorite pasta
Freshly grated parmesan cheese, for serving
Fresh basil leaves for serving

Directions
1. Warm the olive oil in a large heavy bottomed saucepan over medium heat.
2. Season the beef and veal generously with salt and pepper. Working in batches so the pan is not overcrowded, brown the meat for about 4-5 minutes on each side or until well colored. Remove from pan and set aside.
3. Add more oil if needed and brown the Italian sausages. Remove from pan and set aside.

4. Reduce heat to medium-low, add olive oil if needed and add the onions and garlic to the pan. Sauté until fragrant and tender, about 2-3 minutes. Add the tomato paste and red wine and stir well.

5. Using a mesh strainer over the saucepan and add the tomatoes through the strainer to remove seeds and crush the tomatoes.

6. Add the basil and oregano and season with salt and pepper to taste. Stir a few times with a wooden spoon.

7. Add back the browned beef, veal, and pork sausages to the pan. Stir and let simmer the sauce over low heat for 3 to 4 hours, until the meat is tender.

8. In the meantime, prepare the meatballs. In a bowl, add the ground meats and all remaining ingredients for the meatballs. Mix thoroughly with hands until all the ingredients are well combined.

9. To make even meatballs, use an ice cream scooper to make about 12 well rounded meatballs.

10. After 3 hours, remove the beef and veal shanks from the saucepan and let cool on a plate. When cooled enough, pull and shred the meat from the bones with forks or hands. Put the meat back into the sauce and add the meatballs.

11. Let simmer until the meatballs are cooked through, about 45 minutes.

12. When ready to serve, prepare the pasta according to package directions and add to a pasta serving dish. Pour the sauce over and serve with some freshly grated parmesan on the side. Garnish with basil leaves if desired.

3. Tomato Sauce from the Movie
The Godfather

The Godfather's famous line by Fat Pete, "Leave the gun. Take the cannoli," made Fat Clemenzas a popular restaurant sharing its passion for Italian food. Fat Pete in The Godfather loved cooking Italian food. Whip up this tangy tomato sauce and enjoy it with your favorite pasta.

Serves 8–10 | Prep. time 15 minutes |
Cooking time 1 hour 30 minutes

Ingredients

2 (28-ounce) cans diced Italian tomatoes
2 (6-ounce) cans tomato paste
3 garlic cloves, chopped
3 Italian sausages, grilled and sliced
2 tablespoons olive oil
1 pound meatballs, cooked
1 glass dry red wine
¼ cup sugar, or to taste
Cooked pasta for serving
Parmesan cheese for serving

Directions

1. Heat the oil over medium-low heat in a large saucepan.
2. Add the onion and sauté until fragrant, about 2 minutes. Add the garlic and continue to stir-fry for 1-2 minutes, until fragrant and tender.
3. Add tomatoes and tomato paste; cook while stirring for 5 more minutes.
4. Mix in the meatballs and sausages; add the wine, and sugar and stir to combine.
5. Cover and simmer over low heat for about 1 to 1 hour 30 minutes hours, or until the sauce has thickened.
6. Serve the sauce with the cooked pasta and freshly shredded Parmesan cheese.

4. Cacio e Pepe Pasta Sauce from the Movie Eat Pray Love

Remember the famous line from author Elizabeth Gilbert, "Italians take every ingredient they know and make a feast of it"? This Julia Roberts movie also stars this famous Roman pasta sauce prepared from aged Pecorino Romano and black pepper.

Serves 4 | Prep. time 5–10 minutes | Cooking time 14 minutes

Ingredients
¼ cup olive oil
Salt to taste
1 pound tonnarelli, spaghetti or other pasta
2 teaspoons cracked black pepper
¾ cup finely grated Cacio de Roma
1 cup finely grated Pecorino Romano (divided)

Directions
1. Add salted water and pasta to a large cooking pot and heat over high heat.
2. Cook for 8–10 minutes; drain and set aside the pasta. Reserve 1 cup of liquid from the pot.
3. Heat the oil over medium heat in a medium saucepan or skillet.
4. Add the pepper and stir-cook for 1–2 minutes until fragrant.
5. Add the reserved liquid and bring to a boil.
6. Mix in the pasta and add the Cacio de Roma and ¾ cup of the Pecorino Romano; stir again and cook for 2 minutes.
7. Serve the pasta with the remaining Pecorino Romano.

5. Mac and Cheese from the Movie Soul Food

Soul Food brings alive the importance of family; after all, it is family that keeps everyone together. Enjoy this classic mac and cheese that Big Mama used to make for the whole family on Sunday evenings.

Serves 6 | Prep. time 5–10 minutes | Cooking time 5 minutes

Ingredients
1 pound elbow pasta or other short pasta
2½ cups extra sharp cheddar cheese, cubed
2 tablespoons + 1 teaspoon all-purpose flour
1½ teaspoons salt
½ teaspoon pepper
1½ teaspoons dry mustard
¼ teaspoon grated nutmeg

¼ teaspoon cayenne pepper
¼ teaspoon paprika
⅓ cup grated onion
1½ cups half-and-half
1½ cups heavy cream
⅔ cup sour cream
2 eggs, lightly beaten
1 teaspoon Worcestershire sauce
2½ cups extra sharp cheddar cheese, grated

Directions

1. Cook the pasta in salted water according to package instructions. Drain the water and set aside.
2. Add the pasta and cubed cheddar to a 9×13×2-inch baking dish.
3. Combine the spices, salt, and flour in a mixing bowl. Add the eggs and sour cream and whisk.
4. Mix in the heavy cream, Worcestershire sauce, half-and-half, and onion. Pour the mixture over the pasta. Combine well. Top with the shredded cheddar.
5. Preheat the oven to 350°F. Bake for 30–35 minutes until cooked to satisfaction and all the cheese is melted.

6. Ram-Don, a Noodle dish from the Movie Parasite

In Parasite, the 2020 Oscar-winning sensation from South Korea, a memorable scene is when the housekeeper asks" what the hell is ram-don"? after she gets a phone call telling her to prepare it. Here is the quick version of this dish using "ordinary store-bought" ingredients and not the expansive hanwoo sirloin steak from the movie.

Serves 1-2 | Prep. time 10 minutes | Cooking time 10 minutes

Ingredients
Water
½ tablespoon olive oil
1 (6-8-ounce) New York sirloin strip steak, trimmed and cubed into bite-sized pieces
Salt and pepper
1 packet of Neoguri noodle soup base
1 packet of Chapagetti noodles soup base
1 tablespoon butter or olive oil

Directions
1. Boil some water for the noodles, at least 5 cups.
2. Season the sirloin with salt and black pepper. Add the ½ tablespoon of olive oil and mix well. Let rest for 5 minutes.
3. Melt the butter (or oil) in a skillet over medium-high heat and stir-fry the steak until browned and cooked through, about 2-3 minutes for medium or according to your taste. Remove skillet from heat and place steak on a plate and set aside.
4. In the meantime, add 5 cups of boiling water to a deep skillet or saucepan and add both noodles with their vegetable packets. Bring to a quick boil over high heat and continue cooking for 2-3 minutes until the noodles are tender. Reserve ¾ cup of the cooking water and set aside. Drain the noodles and vegetables in a mesh strainer and set aside.
5. Add the cooking water to the skillet where the beef was cooked and add the two remaining flavoring packets and the oil packet. Stir well. Bring to a quick boil over high heat. Once it boils, add the noodle and stir-fry until the sauce thickens, about 1 minute. Remove from heat and add the reserved steak. Stir to combine and serve warm.

16

7. Shoyu Ramen from the Movie Tampopo

Your search for the world-famous Tampopo ramen noodles is over. Tampopo steams the perfect combo of comedy, food, and sex on the silver screen. This great Japanese flick celebrates the joys of food. This ramen recipe is at the center of this amusing movie. Get ready to savor this notoriously seductive and joyous shoyu ramen.

Serves 2 | Prep. time 5 minutes | Cooking time 8–10 minutes

Ingredients
1 clove garlic, finely chopped
1 teaspoon finely chopped ginger
2 chukamen (raw noodles)
2 cups chicken stock
1 cup kombu dashi soup stock

1 teaspoon sesame oil

1 teaspoon salt

1 teaspoon sugar

1 tablespoon sake

3 tablespoons soy sauce

Topping suggestions

Chopped regular green onion or Japanese green onion

Nori (dried seaweed)

Eggs

Cooked meats or seafood

Radishes and other vegetables

Pepper to taste

Directions

1. Heat the oil over medium heat in a medium saucepan or skillet.
2. Add the garlic and ginger and stir-cook until softened.
3. Add the stocks and bring to a boil.
4. Mix in the soy sauce, sake, salt, and sugar. Strain the soup.
5. Cook the noodles in a saucepan filled with water until softened.
6. Drain and add to the soup mixture.
7. Serve the soup with favorite toppings.

8. Scottish Beef Stew from the Movie Brave

Set in the Scottish Highlands, Brave is one of the greatest Pixar epics. A redheaded princess (Merida) is on a mission to save her family from an evil curse. This beef stew will remind you of all the hard work that she did in the movie along with her identical twin brothers.

Serves 4 | Prep. time 5–10 minutes | Cooking time 1 hour 50 minutes

Ingredients
2 tablespoons unsalted butter
2 tablespoons olive oil
All-purpose flour as required
2½ pounds boneless beef chuck, cut into 1½-inch pieces
Salt and pepper to taste
2 carrots, cut into ½-inch sections

2 celery ribs, cut into ½-inch sections
2 medium onions, cut into ½-inch sections
4 ounces (about 1 cup) rutabaga, peeled and cut into ½-inch sections
2 cups beef stock or low-sodium broth
2 sprigs thyme
2 tablespoons red currant jelly
2 cups dry red wine
1 garlic clove, smashed
1 bay leaf
Skirlie Potato Cakes

Directions
1. Season the beef with salt and pepper. Coat with the flour.
2. Heat the olive oil over medium heat in a large saucepan or deep cast-iron skillet.
3. Add the beef and brown it evenly for 4–5 minutes. Set aside. Cook in batches if needed.
4. In the pan, heat the butter. Add the onion, rutabaga, celery and carrots and stir-cook for 5–7 minutes over medium-low heat until softened and translucent.
5. Mix in the wine and jelly; bring to a boil and scrape the brown bits from the bottom. Stir in the stock and beef. Stir and add the garlic, thyme and bay leaf.
6. Reduce heat to low, cover and simmer for about 1½ hours until the beef is cooked to satisfaction. Transfer the beef to a serving plate.
7. Boil the mixture for 10 minutes until thickened to satisfaction. Mix with the beef, season to taste. Remove the bay leaf and thyme sprig.
8. Serve with the potato cakes on top.

9. Boeuf Bourguignon from the Movie Julie and Julia

The movie Julie and Julia is one of the most-talked about recent food movies. Savor this hearty Boeuf a la Bourguignonne that was the favorite recipe of Julia Child. Julie Powell accidently burnt this recipe to a crisp and had to call in sick so that she could remake this wonderful dish.

Serves 6 | Prep. time 10 minutes | Cooking time 3 hours

Ingredients
6 ounces bacon, sliced into ½-inch pieces
2-3 tablespoons olive oil, divided
3 pounds beef chuck, cut into large pieces
Salt and freshly ground black pepper

1 bouquet garni (2 peeled cloves garlic, 1 bay leaf, 1 sprig
parsley, 1 sprig thyme, and 5 peppercorns, tied in a bundle)
4 cups dry red wine
2 cups beef stock, more if needed
Salt and pepper to taste
1-2 carrots, peeled and diced
2 tablespoons flour
1 tablespoon tomato paste
2 cloves garlic, minced
20-24 pearl onion, blanched and peeled
1 pound white mushrooms, cleaned, trimmed and quartered
3 tablespoons butter, divided
Cooked egg noodles or mashed potatoes for serving (optional)
Chopped fresh parsley

Directions

1. Preheat the oven to 475°F.
2. Add 1 tablespoon olive oil to a large oven safe pot such
    as a Dutch oven. Stir-fry the bacon over medium heat for
    2-3 minutes until golden. Remove bacon from pot to a
    plate; lined with paper towels. Reserve for later use.
3. Pat dry the beef cubes with paper towels and season
    generously with salt and pepper. Add the beef to the pan
    and stir-fry in the bacon grease over medium heat until
    browned on every side. Remove beef and place it with
    the bacon. Set aside.
4. Add olive oil if necessary and stir-fry the diced onion for
    2 minutes until fragrant and tender. Add, carrots and stir-
    fry for another minute. Add reserved beef and bacon.
    Dust with the flour and stir to coat.
5. Place in the oven, uncovered, for 3-4 minutes and stir
    with a wooden spoon. Return to oven for another 3-4
    minutes.
6. Remove from oven and lower oven temperature to 325°F

7. Add the bouquet garni. Cover the meat with the beef stock and wine. Add the tomato paste and garlic and stir to combine.

8. Cover with lid and let cook in the oven for 2½ to 3 hours, until the beef if tender.

9. While the beef is cooking, clean and quarter the mushrooms.

10. Pierce each pearl onion with the tip of a sharp knife. Add pearl onions to a saucepan. Add water to cover half of the onions and add 1 tablespoon butter Season with salt. Bring to a boil on medium-high heat. Lower heat to low and let simmer, covered for 20-25 minutes. Remove from heat and set aside

11. Melt remaining butter in a non-stick skillet and stir-fry the mushrooms until golden. Set aside

12. Once the beef is well cooked, remove the beef and vegetables from the sauce. Remove the bouquet garni and discard.

13. Check sauce thickness. If too thick add some beef broth until it has the right consistency. If the sauce is too liquid, over high heat, let it reduce until it thickens. Taste sauce and adjust seasoning with salt and pepper if needed.

14. Return beef and vegetable to the pot. Add mushrooms and pearl onions. Stir and let cook on low heat for a few minutes until mushrooms and onions are heated through, about 4-5 minutes.

15. Serve over egg noodles or mashed potatoes if desired. Sprinkle each plate with chopped parsley.

10. Marinated Cuban Pork Shoulder from the Movie The Chef

Did you know that a Korean-fusion food truck specially created this Cuban pork recipe for this epic 2014 movie? Enjoy this juicy and tender pork shoulder from the rock star chef Roy Choi.

Serves 8 | Prep. time 20 minutes | Marinating time overnight | Cooking time 3 hours

Ingredients
4 pounds pork shoulder, skinless and boneless

Sauce
2 tablespoons lime juice
¼ cup orange juice
Salt and pepper to taste

Marinade

1 tablespoon orange zest

¾ cup orange juice

¾ cup olive oil

1 cup cilantro, lightly packed

½ cup lime juice

8 cloves garlic

½ tablespoon dried oregano or 1 tablespoon fresh oregano leaves

2 teaspoons ground cumin

¼ cup mint leaves, lightly packed

1 teaspoon salt

1 teaspoon pepper

Directions

1. Blend the marinade ingredients in a blender. Add the marinade and pork to a Ziploc bag; shake well.
2. Refrigerate overnight. Take out and allow to reach room temperature.
3. Preheat the oven to 325°F (162°C). Grease a baking dish or roasting dish with some cooking spray or melted butter.
4. Add the pork, reserving the marinade. Cover with foil. Bake for 2½ hours; remove the foil and set aside.
5. Add the marinade to a saucepan along with 2 tablespoons of the drippings from the baking dish and the sauce ingredients.
6. Heat over medium heat; season with salt and pepper. Simmer for 1 minute.
7. Serve the pork shoulder with the sauce on top.

11. Puerco Pibil from the Movie Once Upon a Time in Mexico

This is the favorite dish of Jonny Depp from Robert Rodriguez's super-hit movie. Relive Agent Sands' memories with this Puerco Pibil.

Serves 10–12 | Prep. time 10–15 minutes | Cooking time 4 hours

Ingredients
½ cup orange juice
½ cup white vinegar
5 pounds pork butt, cut into 2-inch cubes
1 tablespoon whole black pepper
½ teaspoon whole cloves
5 tablespoons annatto seeds
2 teaspoons cumin seeds

8 whole allspice berries
2 dried or fresh habanero peppers, cleaned and minced
(optional)
Juice of 5 lemons
1 shot tequila
8 cloves garlic
2 tablespoons salt

Directions

1. In a mortar and pestle or grinder, make a paste out of the peppercorns, annatto seeds, cumin seeds, allspice, and cloves.
2. In a blender, blend the orange juice, habanero peppers, vinegar, garlic, and salt.
3. Mix the blended mixture with the seed paste. Mix in the tequila and lemon juice.
4. Add the marinade and pork to a Ziploc bag; shake well.
5. Refrigerate for 4–6 hours to marinate.
6. Preheat the oven to 325°F (162°C). Grease a baking dish with some cooking spray or melted butter.
7. Add the pork with the marinade. Cover with foil and bake for 4 hours.
8. Serve warm. Great for tacos.

12. Chicken and Okra Gumbo from the Movie Beasts of the Southern Wild

Hushpuppy from this Oscar-winning movie loves to grill this chicken gumbo every day to give her father a filling meal. Prepare these Beasts of the Southern Wild inspired gumbo made with Cajun seasoning and rotisserie chicken.

Serves 6–8 | Prep. time 10 minutes | Cooking time 2 hours 35 minutes

Ingredients
1 large white onion, diced
2 large celery ribs, diced
2 carrots, peeled and diced
2 green bell peppers, diced
3 cloves garlic, finely chopped

1 cup all-purpose flour
½ cup vegetable oil
6 ounces Andouille links, thinly sliced
2 bay leaves
6 cups chicken stock or low-sodium broth
1 tablespoon ground jerk seasoning or 2 tablespoons prepared jerk paste
1 tablespoon smoked hot paprika
1 tablespoon dried thyme
One 3½-pound rotisserie chicken, meat shredded, and skin and bones discarded
¾ pound okra, sliced ¼ inch thick
2 scallions, thinly sliced
Salt and pepper to taste
Tabasco sauce
Steamed rice for serving

Directions

1. Whisk the flour and vegetable oil in a large cast-iron casserole.
2. Cook the roux in a medium saucepan or skillet over low heat for 1 hour and 15 minutes until deep brown, whisking often.
3. Add the onion, garlic, celery, carrots, and bell peppers; stir-cook for 15–20 minutes until softened and fragrant.
4. Add the stock and whisk well.
5. Add the Andouille, jerk paste, bay leaves, paprika, and thyme; simmer the mixture over low heat for about 45 minutes, stirring periodically.
6. Add the okra and simmer for about 15 minutes until tender.
7. Mix in the chicken and season with salt, pepper, and Tabasco. Remove the bay leaves.
8. Serve with the rice and garnish with the scallions if desired.

13. Cheeseburger from the Movie Pulp Fiction

The famous Kahuna Burger needs no introduction. This burger takes center stage as John Travolta informs Samuel L. Jackson about the quirky "Royale with Cheese". Enjoy this big, pulpy beef burger.

Serves 4 | Prep. time 10 minutes | Cooking time 8–10 minutes

Ingredients
1 pound 85% lean ground beef
1 beefsteak tomato, sliced into ¼-inch-thick rounds
Dill pickle slices for serving
Lettuce for serving
Mayonnaise for serving
Ketchup or your choice of dip

Salt and pepper to taste

4 slices American cheese

4 seeded hamburger buns

Directions

1. Preheat your grill to medium-high.
2. Prepare 4 patties from the ground beef. Season generously with salt and pepper.
3. Cut the buns and spread the mayonnaise over the cut sides.
4. Grill the patties for 3–4 minutes until evenly browned. Flip and add the cheese slice on top; cook for 2–3 minutes until the cheese is melted. Set aside.
5. Grill the buns cut side down for about 1 minute until golden brown and lightly toasted.
6. Add the ketchup and mayonnaise over the cut sides of the buns, followed by the patties and tomato slices.
7. Season with some salt and add the lettuce and pickles on top. On the other cut side, add the condiments and sandwich toppings. Place over the other bun slice and serve fresh.

14. White Castle Sliders from the Movie Harold and Kumar

From crazy adventures to shocking mistakes—what haven't these hungry heroes done to reach White Castle and binge on these sliders! These titular characters eat around 30 sliders to make up for their hard work in getting to White Caste; let's see how many you can eat at once.

Serves 6 | Prep. time 20–30 minutes |
Cooking time 5–10 minutes

Ingredients
2 white onions, diced
6 ounces ground beef
6 potato slider buns
Vegetable oil
6 slices American cheese, trimmed

6 dill pickle chips, or more to taste
Salt

Directions
1. Prepare 6 slider-size rectangular patties from the ground meat. You can blend the ground beef and then prepare the patties for a tighter consistency.
2. Punch 5 holes into each patty; freeze the patties until firm.
3. Heat the oil over medium heat in a medium saucepan or skillet.
4. Once hot, add the onion and stir-cook for 2–3 minutes until softened and translucent.
5. Add the patties over the onions, season with some salt.
6. Add the bun bottoms over the patties (cut side down); place the bun tops over them and allow to steam.
7. Set aside; remove the bun tops and set aside.
8. Invert the burgers onto a plate; add a cheese slice and a single dill pickle over each and then place the bun tops over them. Serve warm.

15. Hot Dogs from the Movie Frankenweenie

These hot dogs are a tribute to this great black-and-white animated movie from Tim Burton. The customized hot dogs from F&W's test kitchen will bring back memories of Sparky—the poor pooch.

Serves 8 | Prep. time 5–10 minutes | Cooking time 0 minutes

Ingredients
8 hot dogs, cooked
8 hot dog buns, toasted
2 teaspoons chopped capers
½ cup mayonnaise
1 tablespoon minced shallot
1 tablespoon chopped dill pickle
1 tablespoon caraway seeds, toasted

8 slices crisp-cooked bacon
4 cups shredded lettuce
1 cup chopped tomatoes
⅓ cup small basil leaves

Directions

1. Add the mayonnaise, dill pickle, caraway seeds, shallot and capers to a large mixing bowl. Whisk to mix well.
2. Arrange the buns and place the hot dogs in them; add the bacon, tomatoes, lettuce, and basil on top. Add the mayonnaise mixture on top. Serve warm.

16. Cup O' Pizza from the Movie The Jerk

Cup dinner was the favorite but unusual supper style of our beloved Jerk—Steve Martin. This Cup O' Pizza is very real and easy to cook in the microwave in just 1 minute. Gather around, its cup pizza time!

Serves 1 | Prep. time 5–10 minutes | Cooking time 1 minute

Ingredients
⅛ teaspoon baking powder
Pinch baking soda
¼ cup all-purpose flour
⅛ teaspoon salt
1 tablespoon olive oil

1 tablespoon marinara sauce

3 tablespoons milk

5 mini pepperonis

½ teaspoon dried Italian herbs

1 generous tablespoon mozzarella cheese, shredded

Directions

1. Grease a mug with some oil. Add the flour, baking soda, baking powder, and salt; stir to combine well.
2. Mix in the milk and oil. Spread the marinara sauce on top. Top with the cheese, pepperoni, and herbs.
3. Microwave for 60–80 seconds or until it rises properly and is bubbling at the top. Serve warm.

17. Ricotta Tomato Pizza from the Movie Mystic Pizza

The real-life Mystic Pizza parlor was the center of attention in this coming-of-age movie. This mystic pizza made Julia Roberts think deeply about her future. Remember her saying "I'm gonna be slingin' pizza for the rest of my life"?

Serves 6 | Prep. time 10 minutes | Cooking time 22 minutes

Ingredients

1 cup (about 4 ounces) grated parmesan
1 cup whole-milk ricotta
1 pound pizza dough
¼ cup olive oil (divided)
Salt and pepper to taste
1 large egg, lightly beaten
1 large tomato, halved
2 pints cherry or grape tomatoes
2 tablespoons oregano leaves

Directions

1. Preheat the oven to 500°F (260°C). Arrange racks in the lower and upper thirds.
2. Combine the parmesan cheese, ricotta cheese, salt and pepper in a bowl, mix in the egg.
3. Place the pizza dough on a baking sheet; drizzle 2 tablespoons of the olive oil over the dough. Roll to make a 16-inch round. Spread the cheese mixture on top, keeping it 1 inch from the border.
4. Add the cherry tomatoes to a rimmed baking sheet. Mix them with the remaining 2 tablespoons of olive oil and season with salt and pepper. Arrange the pizza on the top rack and the cherry tomatoes on the bottom rack; bake for 15 minutes.
5. Take out the tomatoes; bake the pizza for 8 more minutes, until the crust is golden brown.
6. Combine the cherry tomatoes and sliced tomatoes, season with salt and pepper. Serve the pizza with the tomatoes and oregano on top.

18. Fried Green Tomato Grilled Cheese from the Movie Fried Green Tomatoes

Fried green tomatoes add extra cinema flavor to this cheesy grilled sandwich. It has crunchiness and tartness that will make you nostalgic. Love Fried Green Tomatoes! Love grilled cheese!

Serves 4 | Prep. time 10 minutes | Cooking time 10–15 minutes

Ingredients

½ cup flour

2 large eggs, beaten

2–3 medium to large green tomatoes, sliced ¼ inch thick

Salt and cracked pepper to taste

2 tablespoons butter

1–2 cups panko breadcrumbs

Oil for frying

8 slices crusty French bread

8 slices Pepper Jack cheese

Directions

1. Season the tomato slices liberally with salt and pepper.
2. Add the panko, eggs, and flour to three separate bowls. Dip the tomato slices in the flour, then eggs, then panko to coat evenly.
3. Heat 1 inch of oil over medium heat in a medium saucepan or skillet.
4. Add the tomato slices in batches and fry 2 minutes per side until evenly golden.
5. Drain over paper towels, sprinkle with salt.
6. Butter 4 of the bread slices and top with cheese slices.
7. Top with 2 tomato slices and another cheese slice. Top with the remaining bread slices.
8. Heat the sandwiches in a lightly greased saucepan over medium heat. Cook until evenly brown on both sides. Serve warm.

19. Coconut Shrimp from the Movie Forrest Gump

Bubba was so adorable with his never-ending monotone ramble in the Tom Hanks picture Forrest Gump. He named all the possible recipes to prepare from shrimp, which inspired Forrest Gump to start his own shrimp company in honor of his late friend. Enjoy this lovely coconut shrimp recipe to relive this all-time-favorite movie.

Serves 1–2 | Prep. time 10 minutes | Cooking time 2 minutes

Ingredients

Shrimp

¾ cup Hefeweizen beer or similar German-style beer

¼ cup all-purpose flour

½ pound medium raw shrimp, peeled and deveined

¾ cup Bisquick
¼ teaspoon cayenne pepper
¼ teaspoon garlic powder
¼ teaspoon seasoning salt
1 cup shredded coconut
Vegetable oil for frying

Sauce
½ teaspoon Cajun seasoning, or to taste
¼ cup orange marmalade

Directions
1. Rinse the shrimp and pat dry.
2. Add the Bisquick and beer to a mixing bowl. Mix well.
3. To another mixing bowl, add the flour, garlic powder, seasoning salt, and cayenne pepper. Mix well.
4. Add the coconut to another bowl. Dip the shrimp first in the flour mixture, then the beer mixture, and finally the coconut to coat well.
5. In a frying pan, heat the oil and fry the shrimp for 45–60 seconds per side until golden brown. Drain over paper towels.
6. Add the sauce ingredients to a mixing bowl. Mix well.
7. Serve the shrimp with the sauce.

20. Chilean Sea Bass from the Movie Jurassic Park

This Chilean sea bass recipe was on the brink of extinction before Steven Spielberg's record-breaking Jurassic Park made it popular again.

Serves 2–3 | Prep. time 10–15 minutes |
Cooking time 10 minutes

Ingredients
3 Chilean sea bass fillets (or black cod)
2 cups green beans
1 cup cherry tomatoes, halved
1 sweet potato, peeled and spiralized
1 tablespoon rosemary, finely chopped
1 small shallot, finely chopped
3 tablespoons cornstarch
Salt and pepper to taste
½ cup dry white wine
½ cup chicken stock
Chopped parsley
Juice of ½ lemon
2 tablespoons butter
Vegetable oil to deep fry

Directions
1. Combine the cornstarch in a bowl with some water; add the spiralized potatoes and combine well.
2. Heat oil over medium heat in a deep skillet or frying pan.
3. Add the potatoes and deep-fry for 3–5 minutes. Drain over paper towels and season with salt.
4. In a saucepan, par-boil the green beans in water. Place in an ice bath for a few minutes; set aside.

5. Heat oil over medium heat in a medium saucepan or skillet.
6. Add the sea bass (skin side down) and evenly brown on both sides.
7. Heat in the oven at 400°F (204°C) until an internal thermometer reads 135°F. Set aside.
8. In the same pan, sauté the shallots for 1 minute until softened.
9. Add ½ cup of chicken stock and ½ cup of dry white wine. Combine and add the rosemary; simmer until the liquid reduces to half.
10. Add the chopped parsley and the lemon juice. Stir to combine.
11. Add the chilled green beans; stir and season with salt and pepper.
12. Stir and cook the mixture until the beans soften; set aside the beans.
13. Mix in the butter.
14. Add the wine mixture and the beans to a serving plate. Cut the fish into strips and add to the plate; add the tomatoes and sweet potatoes on top. Serve warm.

21. Tuna and Butter Lettuce Wraps from the Movie Life of Pi

This stunning movie beautifully captures the unlikely journey of a tiger and Pi. The pair face deadly starvation after being marooned on a lifeboat, then secure a tuna to save their lives. Enjoy these tuna lettuce wraps from the Oscar-winning Life of Pi.

Serves 4 | Prep. time 5–10 minutes | Cooking time 5 minutes

Ingredients
6 tablespoons bottled yuzu ponzu sauce
½ cup soy sauce
¼ cup sugar
1-inch piece ginger, sliced ⅛ inch thick
Juice of 1 orange
Juice of 1 lemon
⅓ cup lime juice
Vegetable oil for frying
1 small package noodles (such as mung bean noodles)
12 leaves butter lettuce
Toasted sesame oil to drizzle
Pinch of salt
12 paper-thin slices of jalapeno, soaked in ice water
9 ounces sushi-grade ahi tuna, cut into 12 slices
Sriracha chili sauce to garnish

Directions
1. Combine the soy sauce, lemon juice, sugar, ginger, yuzu ponzu sauce and orange juice in a medium saucepan or skillet.
2. Simmer the mixture over medium heat to dissolve the sugar. Remove from pan and set aside to cool.

3. In the pan, heat 1½ inches of oil over medium high heat. Fry the noodles for 30 seconds (flip in between) until puffed. Drain over paper towels.
4. Add the sesame oil over the noodles and season with salt. Break the noodles into 1-inch pieces.
5. Arrange the lettuce leaves and top with 2 tablespoons of noodles.
6. Arrange the tuna slices and top with ¼ cup of the sauce. Set aside for 1 minute. Flip the slices and wait for another minute.
7. Over each lettuce leaf, add a tuna slice and another ¼ teaspoon of sauce. Garnish with a drop of Sriracha, a jalapeno slice, and a cilantro sprig; serve warm.

22. Creamy Oyster Stew from the Movie Lincoln

Nominated for 12 Academy Awards, this movie won millions of hearts not just for its incredible screenplay, but also for this steamy, creamy oyster stew, which was Abraham Lincoln's favorite.

Serves 8 | Prep. time 15–20 minutes | Cooking time 40 minutes

Ingredients
1 fennel bulb, cored and finely diced, stems finely chopped
1 quart heavy cream
2 small leeks, white and pale green parts only, thinly sliced
1 large rosemary sprig
8 (1-inch-thick slices) brown bread
3 tablespoons unsalted butter

1 cup frozen baby peas, thawed
30 shucked oysters, with their juices
Salt and pepper to taste
2 tablespoons minced chives
1 teaspoon finely grated lemon zest
2 tablespoons lemon juice

Directions

1. Heat the butter and rosemary over medium heat in a medium saucepan or skillet. Cool down and remove the rosemary.
2. Brush the bread slices with the prepared butter. Place on a baking sheet.
3. Preheat the oven to 350°F (176°C). Bake for 7–8 minutes to toast evenly.
4. Heat the cream and fennel stems over medium heat in a large saucepan. Bring to a boil.
5. Simmer the mixture over low heat for about 20 minutes.
6. Remove the stems and strain the cream.
7. Add the cream to the pan, mix in the diced fennel bulb. Simmer the mixture for about 8–10 minutes.
8. Add the leeks and simmer for 2 minutes.
9. Bring the mixture to a boil, mix in the lemon juice, zest and peas.
10. Remove from heat; stir in the oysters with their liquid. Set aside for 1–2 minutes. Season to taste with salt and pepper.
11. Add to serving bowls, top with the toasted bread and chives. Serve warm.

23. Scallop with Saffron Sauce from the Movie No Reservations

Heard of the famous German movie Mostly Martha? No Reservations is the English remake of that great movie. Set in New York City, this scallop recipe is a signature dish to re-create and share.

Serves 4 | Prep. time 10 minutes | Cooking time 5 minutes

Ingredients
½ teaspoon dried oregano
2 tablespoons lemon pepper
½ cup all-purpose flour
2 teaspoons seasoning salt
2 tablespoons olive oil
¼ cup parsley

4 teaspoons lemon juice
16 sea scallops, rinsed and drained

Sauce
1–2 tablespoons heavy cream
1 stick cold butter, cut into pieces
½ cup finely minced shallots
1 pinch saffron threads
½ cup dry white wine
Fresh lemon juice
Salt and white pepper to taste

Directions
1. Add the flour, thyme, salt, oregano and lemon pepper to a mixing bowl. Mix well. Add the scallops and coat them.
2. Heat the oil over medium heat in a medium saucepan or skillet.
3. Add 4 scallops and sear 2 minutes per side. Set aside and repeat with the remaining scallops. Toss the scallops with the parsley and lemon juice.
4. Heat the wine and shallots in a medium saucepan or skillet over medium heat.
5. Cook until the mixture is reduced to 2 tablespoons. Mix in the cream and saffron threads.
6. Mix in the butter and stir to melt. Do not boil the mixture. Mix in the lemon juice, season with salt and white pepper.
7. Serve the scallops with the sauce on top.

24. Corn Potato Boiled Lobsters from the Movie Annie Hall

Fans of this hilarious comedy will always remember the boiled lobsters. Diane and Woody Allen made everyone chuckle when they wrangled lobsters before cooking.

Serves 4 | Prep. time 5–10 minutes | Cooking time 20 minutes

Ingredients
4 live lobsters (1¼ pounds each)
1½ pounds small Yukon Gold potatoes
4 ears of corn, shucked and halved
1 large onion, quartered
2 heads unpeeled garlic, halved crosswise
½ cup salt
Drawn butter

Directions

1. Fill a large cooking pot to ⅔ capacity with water and heat over high heat.
2. Add the garlic, onion, salt, and potatoes; cover and bring to a boil.
3. Reduce to medium heat; cook for about 10 minutes to soften the potatoes.
4. Add the lobsters; cover and simmer for about 5–6 minutes until the shells are red.
5. Add corn and cook for 3 minutes.
6. Set aside the lobsters, corn, and potatoes; remove the garlic and onions.
7. Clip the claws of lobsters. Serve with the corn, potatoes and drawn butter.

25. Mashed Potatoes from the Movie Lord of the Rings' The Two Towers

Hungry and tired Sean Astin wished for "taters", but all he got was these mashed "Po-tay-toes". Relive these simple yet delicious mashed potatoes from the Oscar-winning Lord of the Rings trilogy.

Serves 6 | Prep. time 5–10 minutes | Cooking time 12 minutes

Ingredients
¼ cup (½ stick) unsalted butter, cut into pieces
2 pounds Yukon Gold potatoes, peeled and cut into ½-inch pieces
Salt and pepper to taste
1–1¼ cups milk, warmed

Directions

1. Add the potatoes to a large cooking pot with salted water to cover.
2. Bring to a boil over high heat.
3. Reduce heat to low, cover and simmer for about 12 minutes until the potatoes are tender.
4. Drain and mash the potatoes to the desired texture.
5. In the cooking pot, heat the butter over medium heat.
6. Add the potatoes and stir-cook for 1 minute until they turn stiff. Mix in the milk and season with salt and pepper. Serve warm.

26. Classic French Ratatouille from the Movie Ratatouille

Ratatouille is a traditional French stewed vegetable dish that made it to the silver screen in the hilarious, touching movie of the same name. Who can help adoring the cute rat Remy that was the secret behind Linguini's mouthwatering recipes?

Serves 12 | Prep. time 15–20 minutes | Cooking time 65 minutes

Ingredients
2 medium red bell peppers, seeds, and ribs removed, cut into ¾-inch pieces
5 cloves garlic, minced
½ cup olive oil (divided)
1 medium white onion, chopped (1½ cups)
2 cups dry white wine

1 tablespoon tomato paste

4 medium tomatoes, quartered

2 medium eggplants, peeled and cut into ½-inch cubes

Salt and pepper to taste

2 sprigs flat-leaf parsley

2 sprigs thyme

3 large basil leaves

4 fresh bay leaves

4 medium zucchinis, cut into ¼-inch rounds

Directions

1. Heat ¼ cup of the olive oil over medium heat in a large cooking pot.
2. Add the onion and bell peppers and stir-cook for 10–12 minutes until softened.
3. Add the tomato paste and garlic; stir-cook for about 1 minute.
4. Add the remaining ¼ cup of olive oil and the eggplant and stir-cook for 8 minutes until softened.
5. Mix in the tomatoes and wine, season with salt and pepper.
6. Bring the mixture to a boil; scrape the brown bits off the bottom.
7. Add the zucchini and herbs; stir-cook for 40–45 minutes over medium heat until the veggies are tender.
8. Serve with the drizzle of olive oil and basil leaves.

27. Pickled Vegetable Egg Salad from the Movie Amour

This historic French movie touched millions of hearts with its emotional plot. This simple yet flavor-rich egg salad will make you revisit the sad twist of events when the elderly couple eats this simple salad.

Serves 4 | Prep. time 5–10 minutes | Cooking time 10 minutes

Ingredients
4 small white turnips, peeled and thinly sliced
4 small red beets, peeled and thinly sliced
4 small golden beets, peeled and thinly sliced
8 small radishes, thinly sliced
2 celery ribs, peeled and thinly sliced crosswise
1 fennel bulb, halved, cored and thinly sliced
3 tablespoons white balsamic vinegar
3 tablespoons olive oil
4 large eggs
Salt and pepper to taste
8 (½-inch-thick) baguette slices, toasted
Fleur de sel to sprinkle

Directions
1. Arrange the vegetables in separate piles over 2 large rimmed baking sheets.
2. Add the vinegar, olive oil, salt, and pepper to a mixing bowl. Whisk to mix well. Top the vegetable piles with the dressing. Set aside for 30–60 minutes.
3. Boil water over medium heat in a large cooking pot or deep saucepan.
4. Add the eggs and boil for 6 minutes; take out and peel the shells.

5. Add cold water to the pan and then add the eggs. Heat the pan again for 2 minutes. Drain and pat the eggs dry; divide into halves.
6. Add the toast slices and egg halves over the vegetable piles; add the fleur de sel on top; serve fresh.

28. Omelet from the Movie Big Night

We pay homage to this classic Italian omelet from the superhot flick Big Night. This simply cooked egg omelet reunites the two immigrant brothers. Let's honor their triumph with this special omelet.

Serves 1 | Prep. time 5–10 minutes | Cooking time 2 minutes

Ingredients
1 teaspoon water
⅛ teaspoon salt
3 large eggs, room temperature
1 tablespoon coarsely chopped mixed herbs (such as flat-leaf parsley, chives, tarragon, chervil, etc.)
1 tablespoon unsalted butter (divided)
Pepper to taste

Directions

1. Cut half the butter into small cubes; set aside the other half.
2. Whisk the eggs in a mixing bowl. Add the water and salt; mix well.
3. Add the cubed butter and herbs; whisk well.
4. Heat the remaining butter over medium heat in a medium saucepan or skillet.
5. Add the egg mixture and cook until the eggs are set. Spread the egg mixture into a thin layer using a fork, work around the edges. Cook for 25–30 seconds.
6. Transfer the omelet to a serving plate; invert and allow the residual heat to cook it for a while.
7. Season with some herbs and pepper; serve warm.

29. Portion Bread from the Movie Star Wars' The Force Awakens

Rey receives her portion in Star Wars: The Force Awakens and adds liquid to instantly transform it into bread. Now it's your turn to recreate this magical portion bread, which takes only 1 minute to get ready.

Serves 1 | Prep. time 5 minutes | Cooking time 1 minute

Ingredients

1½ tablespoons sugar
2 tablespoons whole milk
¼ teaspoon vanilla extract
½ teaspoon matcha powder
¼ teaspoon baking powder
½ teaspoon vegetable oil
¼ cup cake flour
Pinch of salt

Directions

1. Grease a ramequin with some oil.
2. Add the cake flour, salt, sugar, baking powder, and matcha powder to a small bowl. Stir to combine well.
3. Mix in the vanilla and milk. Pour batter into the prepared ramequin.
4. Microwave for 45 seconds or until evenly golden and cooked through. Add more time by increments of 15 seconds, if needed.
5. Serve warm.

30. District 11 Bread from the Movie Hunger Games

Foods from Hunger Games played a vital role in the success of this epic movie. This bread recipe brings back the touching memories of Hunger Games, where people can't afford to feed themselves. Let's pay tribute to this classic piece of cinema with this district bread.

*Yield 16 | Prep. time 20–30 minutes |
Cooking time 12–15 minutes*

Ingredients
¾ cup very warm milk
2¼ teaspoons yeast
2⅓ cups whole wheat flour
1 teaspoon pure honey

1 tablespoon olive oil

1 egg, beaten

1 teaspoon salt

1 tablespoon poppy seeds

½ cup sugar

Sesame seeds for garnish (optional)

Directions

1. Add the warm milk, honey, yeast and ⅓ cup of the flour to a mixing bowl. Mix well.
2. Add another 1 cup of the flour and combine well; add the egg, olive oil, salt, and poppy seeds. Beat the mixture well and add the remaining flour; combine again.
3. Lightly dust your work surface with flour; knead the flour mixture for 8–10 minutes to make a springy, smooth dough. Coat the dough with olive oil and place in a bowl; cover the bowl and set aside for 1 hour to rise and settle.
4. Preheat the oven to 375°F (190°C). Grease a baking sheet with some cooking spray, olive oil, or melted butter.
5. Punch down the dough and divide it into 2 parts. Roll them into 12-inch circles and divide each into 8 wedges. Roll up each wedge, starting from the rounded edge.
6. Arrange on the greased baking sheet and curve into crescent shapes. Top with some sesame seeds, if desired. Bake for 12–15 minutes until golden brown.
7. Serve warm.

31. Cheese Scuffles from the Movie Beauty and the Beast

Beauty and the Beast is one of those rare fairytale classics that is equally adored by children and adults. This cheese scuffle recipe is in the honor of this classic flick from Walt Disney.

Serves 4–6 | Prep. time 10–20 minutes | Cooking time 40 minutes

Ingredients
2 tablespoons grated parmesan
3 tablespoons butter
3 tablespoons all-purpose flour
⅛ teaspoon salt
1 teaspoon dry mustard
½ teaspoon garlic powder

6 ounces sharp cheddar, grated
5 egg whites
½ teaspoon cream of tartar
1⅓ cups milk, hot
4 large egg yolks

Directions

1. Add the flour, salt, dry mustard and garlic powder to a mixing bowl. Mix well.
2. Grease an 8-inch soufflé mold or ramekins with some butter. Add the parmesan to cover the sides. Wrap with plastic and freeze for 5 minutes.
3. Preheat the oven to 375°F (190°C).
4. Heat the butter over medium heat in a medium saucepan or skillet.
5. Add the flour mixture and cook for 2 minutes. Mix in the milk and boil over high heat. Remove from heat.
6. Whisk the eggs yolks in a mixing bowl. Combine with the flour mixture.
7. Add the cheese and whisk again.
8. In another mixing bowl, whisk the eggs whites and cream of tartar. Add ⅓ of this mixture to the base, then keep adding and mixing the white mixture by thirds.
9. Pour the mixture into the ramekins or mold. Keep space of ½ inch from the top.
10. Bake for 35 minutes; serve warm.

32. Homemade Raisin Bran from the Movie Silver Linings Playbook

Bradley Cooper stars in this romantic yet dark and quirky comedy. This multi-grain cereal features in a hilarious scene in which Bradley and Tiffany go out to dinner and Bradley orders Raisin Bran. Tiffany asks why and he replies, "I ordered Raisin Bran because I didn't want there to be any mistaking it for a date." Tiffany provides the smart reply, saying, "It can still be a date if you order Raisin Bran."

Serves 4 | Prep. time 30 minutes | Cooking time 32-36 minutes

Ingredients
Dry ingredients
2 cups wheat bran, unprocessed
1 cup whole wheat flour

1 cup unbleached flour
½ cup nonfat dry milk powder
1 teaspoon salt

Wet ingredients
¾ cup water
¼ cup safflower oil
2 tablespoons honey

2 cups raisins

Directions
1. Preheat oven to 350°F. Line two large baking sheets with parchment paper or generously grease with butter or cooking spray.
2. Mix all the dry ingredients in a large bowl.
3. Whisk together the wet ingredients in another bow.
4. Add the wet ingredients to the dry ingredients and stir to combine well with a wooden spoon until a dough forms into a sticky ball.
5. Cut the dough in 4 even pieces. To roll out the dough, place each piece of dough on a floured waxed paper and cover with another wax paper. Roll out each into a ¼-inch thick rectangle. Remove the top waxed paper and reverse the dough onto the prepared baking sheet. Peel off the waxed paper and repeat for the other dough pieces.
6. Place the first baking sheet in the middle rack of the oven and bake for 16-18 minutes. Repeat with the second baking sheet. Let cool completely before breaking out into small pieces. To do this, you can break some pieces of the cooked bran "cookie" into a large resealable bag or between waxed papers. And with a rolling pin break into smaller cereal bite-sized pieces similar to Raisin bran.
7. Place the broken-up cereal into a large airtight container and add raisins stir to combine. Serve in a bowl with cold milk.

33. French Toasts from the Movie Kramer vs. Kramer

The tragedy of Meryl Streep leaving Dustin Hoffman is hard to watch. Credit to Dustin Hoffman for giving Oscar-winning performance in this epic movie. He also prepared this buttery French toast for his son.

Serves 6 | Prep. time 5–10 minutes | Cooking time 30 minutes

Ingredients
1½ teaspoons finely grated orange zest
2 tablespoons orange juice
1¼ cups whole milk
6 large eggs
2½ tablespoons Grand Marnier or another orange-flavored liqueur (optional)

1 tablespoon sanding sugar

Coarse salt

3 tablespoons unsalted butter + some more (divided)

6 tablespoons sunflower oil (divided)

1 (1¼-pound) loaf brioche, cut into ½-inch slices

Maple syrup or sugar for serving

Directions

1. Whisk the eggs in a mixing bowl. Mix in the sugar, liqueur, a pinch of salt, and the orange juice and zest. Mix in the milk and set aside.
2. Heat 2 tablespoons of the butter and 4 tablespoons of the oil over medium-low heat in a large skillet.
3. Coat the brioche slices with the mixture and add to the skillet; stir-cook for 4–5 minutes per side over medium-low heat. Do not overcrowd the skillet and cook in batches, if needed.
4. Transfer to serving plates.
5. Top with the butter and maple syrup and serve warm.

SWEET RECIPES

34. Snow Cone from the Movie Monsters, Inc.

The Abominable Snowman gifted the world this icy lemon treat. The monsters surely loved having these yellow cones. Make these sweet snow cones from Disney's epic hit movie Monsters, Inc.

Serves 8-12 | Prep. time 5–10 minutes | Cooking time 0 minutes

Ingredients
1 cup lemon juice (6 lemons)
2 cups sugar

2 tablespoons corn syrup
¼ cup water
Yellow food coloring gel
Ice
Cones or bowls for serving

Directions
1. In a medium saucepan or skillet over medium heat, simmer the water, lemon juice, sugar, and corn syrup; whisk well.
2. Stop heating and add the food coloring; stir well and cool down the mixture.
3. Shave the ice (you can use an ice machine) and add to a bowl; add the mixture over it, reserve some of it.
4. Scoop the ice into cup cones or bowls and add some more syrup on top.

35. Chocolate Truffles from the Movie Chocolat

This great classic movie portrays a memorable combination of political uprising, romance, and lust on the silver screen. Get a glimpse of the taste of life's little passions with these rich chocolate truffles.

Ingredients

½ teaspoon salt

1 cup unsalted butter, softened

½ cup superfine sugar

2½ cups rolled oats

2 ounces bittersweet chocolate, melted

2 tablespoons brewed espresso or dark coffee, cooled down

6 tablespoons unsweetened cocoa powder

2 teaspoons vanilla extract

1 cup unsweetened dried coconut, finely shredded

Directions

1. Combine the butter, sugar, and salt in a bowl.
2. Add the cocoa powder, chocolate, espresso and vanilla; combine well. You can also use a hand-mixer.
3. Pulse the oats in a food processor until finely chopped.
4. Mix the oats with the chocolate mixture. Refrigerate for 1 hour.
5. Prepare 36 1-inch truffles. Coat with the coconut and place on a baking sheet.
6. Refrigerate for 2 hours. Serve chilled.

36. Apple Strudel from the Movie
Inglorious Bastards

Inglorious Basterds is not a foodie movie, but this apple strudel surely anchored an excruciating scene between Melanie Laurent (whose family was accidently slaughtered) and Christoph Waltz.

Serves 4–6 | Prep. time 20–30 minutes |
Cooking time 60 minutes

Ingredients
2 egg whites
¼ teaspoon salt
½ tablespoon lemon juice
1½ cups bread flour
¼ cup vegetable oil
¼ cup warm water

4 Granny Smith apples, peeled and chopped
½ cup raisins
Zest of 1 lemon
½ cup sugar
1 tablespoon cinnamon
2 tablespoons melted butter
½ cup hazelnuts and walnuts, finely chopped
1 egg, beaten

Cream
1 tablespoon sugar
1 cup heavy cream

Directions
1. Add the flour, salt, egg whites, lemon juice and oil to a mixing bowl. Mix well.
2. Add warm water and stir the mixture well.
3. Lightly dust your work surface with flour; add the dough and knead to make a springy, smooth dough. Set aside in a bowl for 30 minutes to settle.
4. To another mixing bowl, add the apples, raisins, lemon zest, sugar, and cinnamon. Mix well. Set aside for 30 minutes.
5. Roll the dough to make a 20–24-inch circle. Tug the edges and cut off any rough edges.
6. Brush with the butter and sprinkle with the chopped nuts.
7. Add the apples over one edge of the dough. Roll the dough up.
8. After rolling it completely, seal the edges.
9. Preheat the oven to 350°F (176°C). Grease a baking sheet lined with parchment paper with some cooking spray or melted butter.
10. Add the strudel and brush with beaten egg.
11. Bake for 55–60 minutes until evenly brown; brush with the butter 4–5 times during cooking.
12. Combine the sugar and cream in a bowl. Spoon over the strudel and serve warm.

37. Empire Cookies from the Movie Brave

Pixar has brought us many great animated movies; Brave is one of them. The beloved characters from the movie loved to feast on these Empire Cookies. It's not the worst idea to ditch the popcorn and have these cookies for snacking during reruns of this movie.

Serves 8 | Prep. time 15 minutes | Cooking time 20 minutes

Ingredients
1 cup sugar
1 teaspoon vanilla extract
1 cup powdered sugar, sifted
3 tablespoons milk
⅔ cup unsalted butter, softened
2¾ cups all-purpose flour, sifted

Pinch of salt
Glace cherries, halved
Strawberry or raspberry jam

Directions

1. Preheat the oven to 350°F.
2. Add the sugar and butter to a mixing bowl. Mix well. Add the sifted flour in 2–3 parts, combining to form a dough.
3. Lightly dust your work surface with flour. Roll the dough out to ¼ inch thick. Cut into 3-inch rounds with a cookie cutter.
4. Grease a baking sheet lined with parchment paper with some cooking spray or melted butter.
5. Arrange the rounds on the sheet and refrigerate for 15 minutes.
6. Bake for 15–20 minutes until golden brown. Cool down for a while.
7. Add the milk and powdered sugar to a mixing bowl. Whisk to mix well.
8. Glaze half the cookies with the icing mixture. Keep ¼ inch from the cookie border.
9. Place a cherry half over each cookie; press gently.
10. Add the jam over the remaining cookies; place under the iced cookies to make sandwiches.

38. Beignets from the Movie The Princess and the Frog

It's time to treat yourself to Tiana's favorite beignets from the Disney classic The Princess and the Frog. Beignets from the movie are a reference to the food culture of New Orleans.

Serves 4 | Prep. time 5–10 minutes | Cooking time 1 minute

Ingredients
½ teaspoon baking soda
2 teaspoons baking powder
½ teaspoon salt
2¾ cups flour
1 cup buttermilk

⅓ cup water
⅓ cup sugar
½ teaspoon nutmeg
1 egg, beaten
½ teaspoon vanilla extract
Vegetable oil and confectioners' sugar as required

Directions
1. Add the flour, sugar, nutmeg, salt, baking powder and baking soda to a large mixing bowl. Whisk to mix well.
2. To another mixing bowl, add the egg, buttermilk, water, and vanilla extract. Whisk to mix well.
3. Combine the two mixtures and mix well to form a dough.
4. Dust your work surface with flour. Knead the dough into a ½-inch-thick square. Slice into 2½-inch squares.
5. Heat oil in a deep-frying pan; drop in 3 squares at a time and fry for 3 minutes until evenly golden. Flip and fry for 3 more minutes.
6. Cool down and sprinkle the confectioners' sugar on top; serve warm.

39. Peach Cobbler from the Movie Gone with the Wind

Based on Margaret Mitchell's Gone with the Wind, this classic 1939 movie put this mouthwatering peach cobbler on the silver screen. Get nostalgic and give yourself a historical romance kick with this peach cobbler.

Serves 12 | Prep. time 15 minutes | Cooking time 45 minutes

Ingredients
2½ tablespoons cornstarch
6–8 large ripe peaches, peeled and sliced
¾–1 cup sugar

Crust

¼ cup butter, melted
1 teaspoon baking powder
1 cup all-purpose flour
1 cup sugar
2 large egg whites, beaten
2 large egg yolks

Directions

1. Preheat the oven to 375°F (190°C). Grease a 13×9-inch baking dish with some cooking spray or melted butter.
2. Add the peaches, sugar, and cornstarch to a mixing bowl. Mix well.
3. Transfer the mixture to the baking dish.
4. Add the sugar, flour, butter, egg yolk and baking powder to a mixing bowl. Mix well.
5. Mix in the egg whites and pour over the peaches.
6. Bake for about 45 minutes until the crust is golden brown. Serve warm.

40. Apple Pie from the Movie When Harry Met Sally

Meg Ryan rose to fame with her stunning appearance in When Harry Met Sally. She knew what she wanted in that movie, and now you know what you want—a creamy, delicious apple pie...

Serves 8 | Prep. time 20 minutes | Resting time 60 minutes | Cooking time 65 minutes

Ingredients

<u>Apple filling</u>

3 pounds (about 6) Granny Smith apples, peeled, cored, and sliced

2 tablespoons freshly squeezed lemon juice

1 cup white or brown sugar

Pinch salt

2 tablespoons flour

½ teaspoon cinnamon

¼ teaspoon nutmeg

<u>Crust ingredients</u>

2 cups all-purpose flour

2 tsp white sugar

⅓ cup unsalted cold butter

⅓ cup vegetable shortening, chilled, plus some more for greasing

1 tsp salt

6 tbsp ice water

1 egg, lightly beaten with 1 tbsp of water

Preparation

1. Toss the apples with the lemon juice, sugar, salt, flour, cinnamon, and nutmeg in a bowl. Be sure to coat the apple slices as evenly as possible.
2. To make the pie crust, place the flour, sugar, and salt in a food processor. Add the water, butter, and shortening. Pulse until a ball of dough forms.
3. Remove the dough from the food processor and separate it into two equal portions. Cover in plastic wrap. Place in the refrigerator for 60 minutes before rolling out.

4. Grease generously a 9-inch pie dish.

5. When the dough is well chilled, place it on a working surface lightly floured. Roll out the 2 dough balls into 2 thin circles of about 12 inches.

6. Preheat the oven to 425°F and place the oven rack in the middle position.

7. Place one of the rolled-out dough circles in the greased pie dish. Brush some egg wash on top of the pie edges to help seal the top crust.

8. Scoop the pie filling into the pie dish.

9. For the top crust layer, cut a few vent holes.

10. Place on the top of the filling. Brush the crust lightly with the egg wash. Press down on the edge of the pie to seal both crusts together. Trim the excess.

11. Place the pie on a baking sheet in the preheated oven. Bake for 20 minutes. Reduce the oven heat to 375°F and continue baking for 45 minutes.

12. Remove the pie from the oven, and let it cool down before serving on a wired rack.

13. Serve with a generous scoop of vanilla ice cream.

41. Homemade Twinkies from the Movie WALL-E

Twinkies from this emotional comedy movie always make us remember the cute WALL-E and his cockroach friend who loved binging on Twinkies.

Yield 16 | Prep. time 5–10 minutes | Cooking time 20 minutes

Ingredients
Cake
5 large eggs, white and yolks separated
1 pinch cream of 1 tablespoon vanilla extract
¼ teaspoon salt
½ teaspoon baking powder
1 cup granulated sugar
1 cup cake flour

Filling

¼ cup water
¾ cup granulated sugar
1 teaspoon vanilla extract
1 tablespoon light corn syrup
3 large egg whites
1 pinch cream of tartar

Directions

1. Preheat the oven to 375°F. Grease two mini cake pans for twinkies with some cooking spray or melted butter.
2. Whisk the egg whites in a mixing bowl until peaks form.
3. Whisk the yolks and vanilla in another bowl.
4. Add the salt, baking powder and sugar into the yolk mixture.
5. Add the flour and combine well.
6. Fold in the egg whites with a spatula until well combined.
7. Add the batter to the pans and fill each cavity to ¾ full and bake until golden brown, about 6-8 minutes. Test doneness with a wooden toothpick, it should come out clean when inserted in the middle of the cake
8. Cool down completely on a wired rack before filling.
9. To a saucepan, add the filling ingredients EXCEPT for the egg whites and the cream of tartar. Warm on low heat and stir until the sugar dissolves. Remove from heat and let cool down.
10. Add the egg whites and cream of tartar to a mixing bowl and beat on high speed until stiff peaks form. You can use a hand-held mixer or a stand mixer with the whisk attachment.
11. Fold-in the egg whites to the filling mixture once it has cooled down. Mix until well combined. The filling should be fluffy.
12. Add the filling to a piping bag with a simple medium-sized round tip. Pipe the filling in the 3 small holes in the middle of each Twinkie. Serve and enjoy!

42. Rapunzel's Cookies from the Movie Tangled

These delicious cookies from Disney's Tangled will make kids fall in love with them. Give these cookies a magical, artistic touch with some colorful frosting, sprinkles, etc. and your kids will simply run for them.

Yield 20–25 cookies | Prep. time 10 minutes | Cooking time 8 minutes

Ingredients
1 cup softened butter
1 egg
¾ cup brown sugar
¾ cup sugar
1½ teaspoons vanilla extract
1 teaspoon baking powder
1 teaspoon baking soda

½ teaspoon salt
2¼ cups flour
Vanilla frosting
¾ pound chocolate chips
Sprinkles
Food coloring (optional)

Directions
1. Add the egg, sugar, butter and vanilla extract to a mixing bowl. Mix well.
2. Add the salt, baking soda, baking powder, and flour. Combine well. Add the chocolate chips and combine again.
3. Form into small balls and place on a greased baking sheet. Keep some space between each ball.
4. Gently flatten into a cookie shape.
5. Preheat the oven to 375°F. Bake for 7–8 minutes until evenly brown. Cool down for a while.
6. Divide the vanilla frosting into 2 or 3 and add a few drops of food coloring to each. Mix well.
7. Generously add frosting to half the cookies and place another one on top to make a sandwich. Squish a bit to get some of the frosting on the edges of the cookie sandwiches. Roll the sandwiches over the sprinkles.

43. Chocolate Sauce from the Movie Willy Wonka and the Chocolate Factory

Give your dessert a movie flavor tonight with this delicious, creamy chocolate sauce straight from Willy Wonka's chocolate factory. This sauce mesmerized the audience, and now it's going to mesmerize you.

Yield 2 cups | Prep. time 5 minutes |
Cooking time 10–15 minutes

Ingredients

2 ounces unsweetened chocolate, chopped
2 ounces bittersweet chocolate, chopped
1 cup sugar
2 egg yolks, lightly beaten
½ cup half-and-half
½ cup butter, melted

Directions

1. Heat the half-and-half and sugar over medium heat in a medium saucepan or skillet.
2. Stir to dissolve the sugar. Mix in the butter and chocolates; set aside to cool.
3. Stir-cook the egg yolk for 3 minutes; cool down and mix with the chocolate sauce.

BEVERAGES AND COCKTAIL RECIPES

44. Butterbeer from the Movies of Harry Potter

If the recipe is from Harry Potter, the chances of it being normal are next to zero. Butterbeer is certainly an unusual drink; but the thrill of making this beer, which was popular among the wizarding population, is simply exhilarating.

Serves 2 | Prep. time 5–10 minutes | Cooking time 2–3 minutes

Ingredients

2 tablespoons whipped butter
1½ cups vanilla cream soda
¼ cup evaporated milk
¼ cup butterscotch sauce
Cinnamon

Directions

1. Combine the butter, butterscotch sauce and milk in an oven-safe bowl.
2. Microwave for 1 minute; mix again to melt the butter completely.
3. Add the cream soda to another oven-safe bowl; microwave for 1½ minutes.
4. Divide the butterscotch mixture into two cold mugs.
5. Add the soda cream on top. Serve with a sprinkle of cinnamon on top.

45. White Hot Chocolate from the Movie Frozen

Is your daughter a fan of Disney's Frozen? Then you can make her day special with this blue hot chocolate. This popular blue hot chocolate from Frozen is still trending among kids.

Serves 2 | Prep. time 5–10 minutes | Cooking time 10 minutes

Ingredients
2 cups milk or half-and-half
4 drops blue food coloring (divided)
1 cup white chocolate chips

¼ cup sugar for rims of glasses
Whipped cream and sprinkles for topping (optional)

Directions

1. Heat the milk or half-and-half in a medium saucepan or skillet over low heat.
2. Add the chocolate chips and stir for 5–10 minutes until they melt.
3. Add 2 drops of the food coloring and stir; remove from heat.
4. Add the sugar and the remaining 2 drops of food coloring to a mixing bowl. Mix well.
5. Coat the rims of the glasses with the sugar mixture and serve the hot chocolate warm. Top with whipped cream and sprinkles if desired.

46. Spiced Hot Dark Chocolate from the Movie Chocolat

When Juliette Binoche opens a chocolate shop in rural France, she's operating in unfriendly territory. This spiced hot chocolate is one of the magical offerings that help her win over the villagers.

Serves 4 | Prep. time 5–10 minutes | Cooking time 5 minutes

Ingredients
6 ounces dark chocolate, chopped
1 quart milk or alternative milk beverages like almond milk or soy milk
⅛–¼ teaspoon ground cardamom, or to taste
½ teaspoon ground cinnamon
⅛ teaspoon cayenne pepper
⅛ teaspoon coarse salt

Directions

1. Add the ingredients to a medium saucepan or skillet and heat over medium heat.
2. Whisk for 4–5 minutes until the chocolate melts.
3. Serve warm.

47. White Russian Cocktail from the Movie The Big Lebowski

No one can argue that it was The Big Lebowski that made this drink highly popular. The White Russian is the drink of choice for the protagonist, "The Dude" Lebowski. Can you count how many times he referred to this drink as a "Caucasian"? Time for a rerun in the company of this drink?

Serves 1 | Prep. time 5 minutes | Cooking time 0 minutes

Ingredients

⅔ ounce Kahlua or other coffee liqueur

1½ ounces chilled vodka

⅔ ounce light cream

Ice cubes

Directions

1. Add some ice cubes to an old-fashioned glass and pour in the other ingredients.
2. Stir gently and serve.

48. Vesper from the Movie Casino Royale

There is no scarcity of James Bond fans. The vesper martini ordered by the British Secret Service agent in Casino Royale is extremely precise in the midst of the thrilling poker game night.

Serves 1 | Prep. time 5 minutes | Cooking time 0 minutes

Ingredients
1 ounce vodka
3 ounces gin
½ ounce dry vermouth
Lemon peel for garnish

Directions
1. Add the ingredients to a cocktail shaker.
2. Shake vigorously to mix well.
3. Strain the mixture into a chilled cocktail glass.
4. Garnish with a lemon peel.

49. Champagne Cocktail from the Movie Casablanca

Relive the romantic tension that flowed at Rick Blaine's Moroccan nightclub in Casablanca by enjoying this sophisticated champagne fizz.

Serves 1 | Prep. time 5 minutes | Cooking time 0 minutes

Ingredients
Angostura bitters
1 cube of white sugar
Champagne, chilled

Directions

1. Place the sugar cube at the bottom of a champagne glass. Add a few drops of Angostura bitter. Cover with champagne. With a spoon, mix until the sugar has dissolved. Add champagne and give it a few stirs.
2. Garnish with a lemon peel strip and serve.

50. Cosmopolitan from the Movie Sex and the City

Sex and the City premiered around 20 years ago; the show, which was later made into a movie of the same name, made the Cosmopolitan famous. When Carrie, Samantha, Charlotte, and Miranda used to hang out at New York nightclubs, this was the drink that accompanied their gossip.

Serves 1 | Prep. time 5 minutes | Cooking time 0 minutes

Ingredients
½ ounce Cointreau (or Grand Marnier)
½ ounce lime juice
1½ ounces vodka
1 ounce cranberry juice
Ice cubes
Orange rind twist for garnish

Directions

1. Add the ice cubes, vodka, cranberry juice, Cointreau and lime juice to a cocktail shaker.
2. Shake vigorously to mix well.
3. Strain the mixture into a chilled cocktail glass. Garnish with an orange rind.

51. Martini from the Movie The Thin Man

Martinis were the special company of the loving duo of Nick and Nora Charles while solving mysteries. Enjoy the special martini from this 1934 detective comedy.

Serves 8 | Prep. time 5 minutes | Cooking time 0 minutes

Ingredients
¼ cup dry vermouth
4 cups vodka or gin
Ice cubes
Cocktail olives, caper berries, or cocktail onions for garnish

Directions

1. Add ½ cup gin or vodka and 1½ teaspoons vermouth to a cocktail shaker.
2. Shake well and strain into chilled cocktail glasses.
3. Garnish with the capers, cocktail onions or olives.
4. Repeat with the remaining ingredients.
5. Serve cold.

APPENDIX

Cooking Conversion Charts

1. Measuring Equivalent Chart

Type	Imperial	Imperial	Metric
Weight	1 dry ounce		28 g
	1 pound	16 dry ounces	0.45 kg
Volume	1 teaspoon		5 ml
	1 dessert spoon	2 teaspoons	10 ml
	1 tablespoon	3 teaspoons	15 ml
	1 Australian tablespoon	4 teaspoons	20 ml
	1 fluid ounce	2 tablespoons	30 ml
	1 cup	16 tablespoons	240 ml
	1 cup	8 fluid ounces	240 ml
	1 pint	2 cups	470 ml
	1 quart	2 pints	0.95 l
	1 gallon	4 quarts	3.8 l
Length	1 inch		2.54 cm

*   Numbers are rounded to the closest equivalent

2. Oven Temperature Equivalent Chart

Fahrenheit (°F)	Celsius (°C)	Gas Mark
220	100	
225	110	1/4
250	120	1/2
275	140	1
300	150	2
325	160	3
350	180	4
375	190	5
400	200	6
425	220	7
450	230	8
475	250	9
500	260	

* Celsius (°C) = T (°F)-32] * 5/9

** Fahrenheit (°F) = T (°C) * 9/5 + 32

*** Numbers are rounded to the closest equivalent

Image Credits

Made in the USA
Middletown, DE
26 July 2022

70042418R00066